SUPER NATURAL BUGS

AWESOME CREATURES AND THEIR SUPER POWERS!

LEON GRAY

WAYLAND

First published in 2013 by Wayland
Copyright © Wayland 2013

Wayland
338 Euston Road
London NW1 3BH

Wayland Australia
Level 17/207
Kent Street
Sydney, NSW 2000

THE BIONIC EARTHWORM
- PAGE 20

THE MURDEROUS WIDOW
SPIDER - PAGE 10

Editor: Nicola Edwards
Designer: Rocket Design (East Anglia) Ltd

Dewey categorisation: 508

ISBN 978 0 7502 7935 2

Printed in China

10 9 8 7 6 5 4 3 2 1

Wayland is a division of Hachette Children's Books,
an Hachette UK company.
www.hachette.co.uk

Picture acknowledgements:
The author and publisher would like to thank the following
for allowing their pictures to be reproduced in this publication:
Pictures by Shutterstock except for p6 John Abbott/Visuals Unlimited, Inc/Science Photo Library; pp 7-9
Wikimedia Commons; p9 (b) CDC/World Health Organization; p10 (t) Shutterstock/Nate Allred; p11 Wikimedia
Commons; p12 Shutterstock/Johann Viloria; p13 (t) Nature Production/naturepl.com, (b) Shutterstock/Johann
Viloria; p14 Wikimedia Commons; p15 (t) Shutterstock/Johan Larson, (b) Wikimedia Commons/Ushaeugene;
p16 Shutterstock/ R.A.R. de Bruijn Holding BV; p17 (t) Shutterstock/ Eric Isselee, (b) Wikimedia Commons/
Adam Matan; p18 Wikimedia Commons/Bruce Marlin; p19 (t) Wikimedia Commons/Duwwel, (b) Shutterstock/
Four Oaks; p20 Shutterstock/ D. Kucharski K. Kucharska; p21 (t) Wikimedia Commons/ Rasbak, (b) Wikimedia
Commons/ Holger Casselmann; p22 Shutterstock/ Injun; p23 (t) Wikimedia Commons/ Plegadis, (b) Wikimedia
Commons/ Pollinator; p24 (t) Shutterstock/ Cosmin Manci, (b) Wikimedia Commons/ Uwe Gille; p25 CDC/Janice
Haney Carr; Wikimedia Commons/ Mnolf; p27 Wikimedia Commons; Wikimedia Commons/ Morkelsker; p29 (t)
James H Robinson/Science Photo Library, (b) Wikimedia Commons/ Ltshears; p30 (t) Wikimedia Commons/ Didier
Descouens; p31 (t) Wikimedia Commons/ Hans Hillewaert, (b) Wikimedia Commons/ Novita Estiti; p32 (t) Nature
Picture Library/ Gavin Maxwell, (b) Shutterstock/ Luca Galuzzi; p33 Vipin Balega; Shutterstock/ Denis Vesely;
p35 Wikimedia Commons (b) Nicomeier; p36 Shutterstock/ kissound; p37 (t) Wikimedia Commons / Alpsdake, (b,
both) Wikimedia Commons / Takahashi; p39 CDC/Frank Collins, PhD / James Gathany; p40 Shutterstock/ Hugh
Lansdown; p41 (both) DARLYNE A. MURAWSKI/National Geographic Creative; p42 Wikimedia Commons; p43
Wikimedia Commons/ Patrick Coin

AWESOME!

CONTENTS

THE 'KISS OF DEATH' ASSASSIN BUG – PAGE 8

THE EXPLOSIVE BOMBARDIER BEETLE – PAGE 12

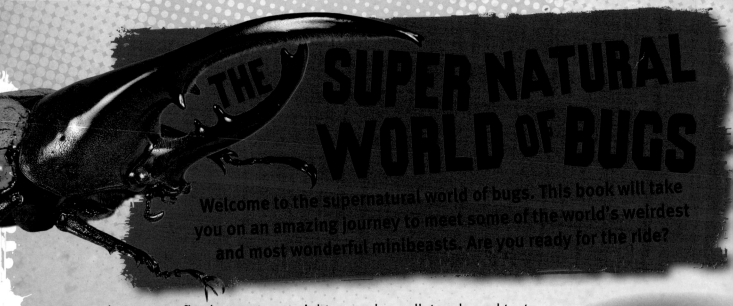

THE SUPER NATURAL WORLD OF BUGS

Welcome to the supernatural world of bugs. This book will take you on an amazing journey to meet some of the world's weirdest and most wonderful minibeasts. Are you ready for the ride?

Every day, we use five key senses – sight, sound, smell, touch, and taste – as we go about our daily lives. Our brains process this information so we can make sense of the world and communicate with others. Bugs and minibeasts have their own ways of sensing the world. Some have sharper sight, stronger smell, super-sensitive touch, or even senses that are completely outside our own experience – so much so that they appear to be supernatural powers!

SUPER SIGHT

Vision helps many bugs find food, move around, and hide from predators. Some bugs have far sharper eyesight than our own and can see things much more clearly. Others see the world completely differently, sensing forms of light that are invisible to the human eye.

FINELY TUNED

Many different bugs have a remarkable sense of hearing and can detect the faintest noises. Others can pick up sounds outside the human range of hearing.

SMELL AND TASTE

Our own smell and taste are weak compared to those of many bugs. A sharp sense of smell helps them to find food, pick up the scent of mates, avoid enemies or sniff their way through unfamiliar places.

SKIN DEEP

Some bugs live in complete darkness all the time – for example, in caves or under the ground. Good eyesight is useless in the dark, so instead these bugs have developed super-sensory touch to feel their way around. Some even have special touch organs, such as antennae and feelers, to help them move around in safety.

SUPER NATURAL POWER!

There are some bugs that have developed incredible supernatural powers outside our own experience. Can you imagine being able to regenerate new arms and legs or freeze solid for months? Some bug superpowers are just plain amazing – such as the ability to boil an enemy alive or spray it with toxic chemicals.

LOOK OUT FOR THESE SPECIAL FEATURES!

CRITTER STATS!

You can find out the key information about each bug in this box feature, such as its typical size, how many species (different types) there are in its group, and in what type of habitat the bug lives.

SUPERHERO STYLE

GET READY TO MEET SOME OF THE COMIC-BOOK CHARACTERS AND ANIMATED ACTION HEROES (AND VILLAINS!) THAT SHARE THE SUPERNATURAL POWERS OF THE BUGS IN THIS BOOK. FIND OUT ABOUT EVERYTHING FROM THE CRYOGENIC SUPERPOWERS OF MR FREEZE TO THE INCREDIBLE REGENERATIVE POWERS OF WOLVERINE.

THE HUMAN FACTOR

THIS BOX WILL EXPLORE SOME OF THE WAYS IN WHICH SCIENTISTS HAVE HARNESSED THE SUPERPOWERS OF BUGS AND MINIBEASTS IN SCIENCE, TECHNOLOGY, MEDICINE AND OTHER AREAS TO MAKE OUR LIVES MUCH EASIER.

THE MIND-CONTROLLING ANT-DECAPITATING FLY

Ant-decapitating flies would be your worst nightmare – if you were a fire ant! These fearsome flies lay their eggs inside the bodies of the ants. When the eggs hatch, the maggots eat the ants from the inside out, eventually munching their way through the victims' brains and turning them into zombie ants!

There are around 110 species of ant-decapitating flies. These fearsome flies live in tropical parts of South America in the same places as the fire ants. Ant-decapitating flies have also been introduced to other parts of the world, including the United States, to control the exploding populations of ants.

CRITTER STATS!

Size: Up to 5 mm
Number of species: 110
Habitat: Tropical South America

THE HUMAN FACTOR

SCIENTISTS CALLED FORENSIC ENTOMOLOGISTS USE THE MAGGOTS OF SOME FLIES TO HELP CONVICT MURDER SUSPECTS. SOME FLIES LAY THEIR EGGS ON HUMAN CORPSES. THE ENTOMOLOGISTS MEASURE THE SIZE AND DEVELOPMENT OF THE MAGGOTS TO DETERMINE HOW LONG THEY HAVE BEEN ALIVE. THIS CAN THEN BE USED TO ESTIMATE THE TIME OF A PERSON'S DEATH.

SUPER NATURAL POWER!

Ant-decapitating flies have the **supernatural power of mind control,** but they achieve this feat in a horribly gruesome way. The female flies constantly buzz around the ant colony, looking for suitable host. She then jumps on the ant, **stabs it with her ovipositor,** and lays an egg inside its body. When the egg hatches, the maggot starts to eat its way through the body of the ant and into its head. Eventually, the growing maggot **munches through the living ant's brain,** effectively turning it into a zombie.

AWESOME!
THIS PICURE SHOWS AN EGG IN A FEMALE FLY'S OVIPOSITOR, SEEN THROUGH AN ELECTRON MICROSCOPE.

BRAINLESS BUGS

A fire ant can survive without a brain because it has a network of nerves running down its back. These nerves **keep the ant in its zombie-like state,** and the maggot continues to feed and grow inside its body. After about two weeks, the maggot releases a chemical called an enzyme. This seeps into muscles in the back of the ant's head and dissolves them, **making the ant's head fall right off!**
Following metamorphosis, the maggot transforms into the adult fly, which emerges from the dead ant.

MEANWHILE, AT THE MOVIES...

SUPERHERO STYLE

SEVERAL COMIC-BOOK CHARACTERS AND SUPERHEROES USE THE POWER OF MIND CONTROL OVER THEIR ENEMIES. THEY INCLUDE:

POISON IVY
HER BODY PRODUCES MIND-CONTROLLING CHEMICAL PHEROMONES TO USE AGAINST ENEMIES.

PURPLE MAN
THIS SUPERVILLAIN RELEASES A CHEMICAL PHEROMONE INTO THE AIR. WHEN INHALED OR ABSORBED THROUGH THE SKIN, IT CAN BE USED FOR MIND CONTROL

FEARSOME FAMILY

Belonging to a large family of phorid flies, ant-decapitating flies have some equally grisly relatives. Coffin flies are particularly gruesome, laying their eggs **on the remains of dead people.** The maggots continue to live inside their human hosts within the buried coffins, which give the flies their common name.

WOW!
THIS ANT HAS LOST ITS HEAD TO AN ANT-DECAPITATING FLY.

THE 'KISS OF DEATH' ASSASSIN BUG

Assassin bugs are a group of predatory insects that certainly live up to their common name. These small but deadly bugs strike with lightning speed to feast on the bodies and blood of animals such as bats, cattle and even people. They inject paralyzing venom into their prey, which then dissolves their victims' bodies from the inside out.

Belonging to a large group of around 4,000 different insect species, these predatory bugs live in many different parts of the world, from Africa and Europe to the Americas. **Assassin bugs are swift, fearless predators** that usually attack and eat other bugs – including members of their own species!

CRITTER STATS!

Size: 4–40 mm

Number of species: More than 4,000

Habitat: Worldwide, especially forests

THE HUMAN FACTOR

SOME ASSASSIN BUGS ARE HELPFUL TO GARDENERS AND FARMERS BECAUSE THEY PREY ON THE INSECT PESTS THAT DESTROY GARDEN PLANTS AND IMPORTANT CROPS.

SUPER NATURAL POWER!

Some assassin bugs have a more sinister side. They are known as 'kissing bugs' because they give people the 'kiss of death'. The bugs target soft parts of the body such as the lips. They use their sharp mouthparts to pierce through the soft skin and inject a chemical that paralyzes the flesh around the bite. The bugs are then free to feast on human blood.

DEADLY DISEASE

Some assassin bugs carry a tiny parasite, which enters the person's bloodstream when the bug bites. This parasite causes a deadly disease called Chagas disease, which is particularly common in Central and South America. In the early stages of the disease, the symptoms are often no more than a mild fever and swelling and pain around the bite. In many cases, these symptoms usually clear up within a few weeks. But people go on to develop permanent heart and digestive conditions, which can be deadly if left untreated.

AWESOME!

THESE BEASTLY BUGS OFTEN LIVE IN PEOPLE'S BEDS AND ATTACK AT NIGHT, WHEN PEOPLE ARE ASLEEP.

MEANWHILE, AT THE MOVIES...

SUPERHERO STYLE

COMIC-BOOK AND ACTION HEROES AND VILLAINS THAT POSSESS THE 'KISS OF DEATH' SUPERPOWER INCLUDE:

THE JOKER IN THE MOVIE 'THE DARK KNIGHT RETURNS', THE JOKER USES TOXIC LIPSTICK TO GIVE HIS OPPONENTS THE KISS OF DEATH.

ROGUE THIS X-MEN CHARACTER DISCOVERED HER 'KISS OF DEATH' SUPERPOWER WHEN SHE KISSED HER BOYFRIEND FOR THIS FIRST TIME - AND PUT HIM INTO A COMA!

WOW!

AFTER PIERCING THE SKIN, AN ASSASSIN BUG PREPARES TO FEAST ON HUMAN BLOOD.

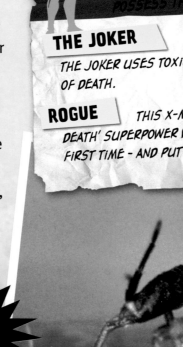

THE MURDEROUS WIDOW SPIDER

Widow spiders are a small group of venomous spiders that live in many different parts of the world, especially North America. It pays to be female if you are a widow spider. Females usually eat the males after mating with them!

There are four species within the group of widow spiders that take the name 'black widow spider'. Three are found in North America and one lives in central Asia and the Mediterranean region of Europe. Like all spiders, they have eight legs and a body divided into two parts – a head and a rear end called an abdomen – and **fang-bearing jaws called chelicerae.**

CRITTER STATS!

Size: Up to 40 mm long

Number of species: 31/32

Habitat: Most habitats around the world

WOW!

THE REDBACK SPIDER IS EASILY IDENTIFIED BY THE RED MARK ON THE BACK OF ITS ABDOMEN.

 THE HUMAN FACTOR

THE REDBACK SPIDER IS A WIDOW SPIDER THAT LIVES IN AUSTRALIA. ITS VENOM IS STRONG ENOUGH TO KILL AN ADULT PERSON – THOUGH CHILDREN AND OLDER ADULTS ARE MOST AT RISK. FORTUNATELY, SCIENTISTS HAVE DEVELOPED AN ANTIVENIN TO REDBACK BITES, SO THESE SPIDERS POSE LESS OF A THREAT THAN THEY ONCE DID. IN FACT, NO ONE HAS DIED FROM A REDBACK BITE SINCE THE ANTIVENIN WAS CREATED IN 1956.

SUPER NATURAL POWER!

Like all widow spiders, the black widow is as deadly to other widow spiders as it is to its prey. Female black widows commit the **ultimate crime of passion** – by eating the males after mating with them. Bizarrely enough, the male may encourage the female to commit her crime by **waving his colourful abdomen near her face** as they mate.

SPINNING SILK

The female – having built up her strength by feasting on her mate – lays around 300 eggs and **spins a cocoon of silk** around them. When the eggs hatch, the young spiders blow away in the wind. They build their first webs where they land.

Adult black widows build huge silk webs to trap prey such as insects and other bugs. The silk is also **strong enough to catch even bigger animals,** such as lizards. The spider then moves in and injects potent venom to paralyse and kill its prey.

AWESOME!
WIDOW SPIDERS SPIN HUGE SILK WEBS AND COCOONS OF SILK IN THE SHAPE OF PING PONG BALLS.

MEANWHILE, AT THE MOVIES...
SUPERHERO STYLE

SEVERAL SUPERHEROES APPEAR IN THE MARVEL COMIC BOOKS WITH THE CODE NAME BLACK WIDOW:

NATALIA ROMANOVA
AN ATHLETIC SOVIET SUPERVILLAIN AND ENEMY OF IRON MAN, WHO LATER DEFECTED TO THE UNITED STATES AND JOINED THE AVENGERS SUPERHERO TEAM.

YELENA BELOVA
THE SECOND BLACK WIDOW, YELENA BELOVA WAS A SOVIET SPY AND ASSASSIN WHO ALSO HAD SUPERHUMAN ATHLETIC ABILITIES.

THE EXPLOSIVE BOMBARDIER BEETLE

These big, bulky beetles live in woodlands or grasslands around the world, with the exception of Antarctica. Most species, of which there are around 500, are ferocious carnivores, including the larvae, and the adults have a secret weapon to protect them from their main enemies – ants.

The bombardier beetle is the ultimate defender. This minibeast may not look like much, but it has a secret weapon – **it's packing heat.** Ants are the bombardier's arch-enemies. They swarm around the beetle, biting and nipping and trying to eat it. But the bombardier beetle has a seriously impressive superpower to help defend him. Well, actually, **it's up his bottom!**

THE HUMAN FACTOR

PEOPLE HAVE BEEN USING TOXIC CHEMICALS TO DEFEND THEMSELVES AND ATTACK THEIR ENEMIES FOR HUNDREDS OF YEARS. FROM MEDIEVAL SIEGES, DURING WHICH SOLDIERS TIPPED BOILING OIL AND INCENDIARY BOMBS ON ADVANCING SOLDIERS, TO MODERN-DAY CHEMICAL NERVE AGENTS, CHEMICAL WARFARE IS THE ULTIMATE DETERRENT ON THE BATTLEFIELD. CHEMICAL WEAPONS HAVE PROVED SO DEADLY THAT MOST COUNTRIES NOW AGREE THEY SHOULD NOT BE USED IN WAR.

Stored within the beetle's abdomen are two powerful liquids that the beetle can mix together, creating a chemical reaction that is so explosive that it sends **a jet of boiling, toxic acid** out of his rear all over attacking ants. The acid smells disgusting, and burns anything it touches. It's so hot that the beetle has to jet it out in pulses of **500 bursts per second** to stop him from burning his own bottom. The force of the explosion forces the liquid out of 'jets' in the beetle's body with a loud pop. The beetle can **swivel its bottom through 360 degrees** to direct the spray with amazing accuracy.

WOW!
THE ACID DISCHARGED BY A BOMBADIER BEETLE IS AS HOT AS BOILING WATER!

MEANWHILE, AT THE MOVIES...

SUPERHERO STYLE

COMIC-BOOK CHARACTERS AND ACTION HEROES WHO USE EXPLOSIVES TO PROTECT THEMSELVES INCLUDE:

NITRO
TURNS HIS BODY INTO A GAS AND EXPLODES WITH A FORCE EQUIVALENT TO HUNDREDS OF KILOGRAMMES OF DYNAMITE.

DAMAGE
RELEASES ENERGY IN THE FORM OF POWERFUL EXPLOSIONS. DAMAGE ACTUALLY STARTED ANOTHER BIG BANG EXPLOSION WHEN ONE OF HIS ENEMIES DESTROYED THE UNIVERSE.

THE 'INVISIBLE' BORNEO STICK INSECT

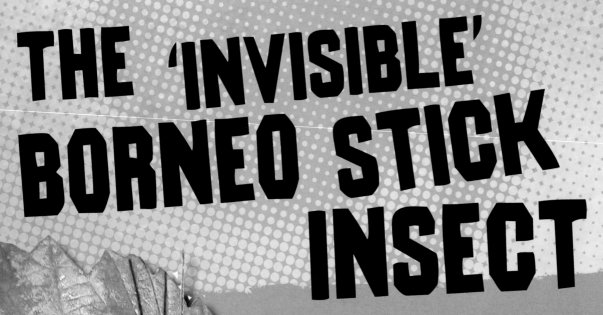

The Borneo stick insect is the longest insect in the world. This slender bug can grow up to half a metre long and hides amongst the dense forest vegetation on an island called Borneo – part of a country called Indonesia. Borneo stick insects may be very long, but they are hard to spot thanks to their amazing camouflage.

Scientists found the longest Borneo stick insect in 2008 during an expedition to the rainforests of Borneo in Southeast Asia. When they measured it, they found it was 56.7 cm long – **about as long as your arm**. The scientists took the (dead) stick insect home to London, where it is on display at the Natural History Museum.

CRITTER STATS!

CRITTER STATS!

Size: Up to 57 cm long
Number of species: 1
Habitat: Dense vegetation

SUPER NATURAL POWER!

Like all stick insects, the Borneo stick insect is **a master of disguise**. It spends most of the day resting in the treetops. It has a long, thin greenish brown body and legs that look exactly like the branches of trees in which they live. To add to the camouflage, stick insects gently rock from side to side **just like branches swaying in the breeze**. At night, the Borneo stick insect becomes active and roams through the dense vegetation to feed on the plentiful supply of leaves.

MEANWHILE, AT THE MOVIES...
SUPERHERO STYLE

COMIC-BOOK CHARACTERS AND ACTION HEROES WHO CAN MIMIC THEIR ENEMIES OR USE CAMOUFLAGE INCLUDE:

AMAZO THIS DC COMICS CHARACTER CAN COPY THE ABILITIES AND SUPERPOWERS OF ANY SUPERHEROES HE MEETS.

NIGHTCRAWLER A MUTANT WITH SUPERHUMAN AGILITY, NIGHTCRAWLER USES CAMOUFLAGE TO BLEND INTO THE SHADOWS AND MOVE AROUND WITHOUT BEING SEEN.

LEAF-LIKE RELATIVES

Stick insects belong to a large group of about 3,000 species that also include leaf insects. These insects are **just as skilled at camouflage**, having green and brown bodies to match the colour of their leafy homes. Some species even have dark blotches and spots to copy the natural discolouration of real leaves.

AWESOME!
AS THEIR NAME SUGGESTS, LEAF INSECTS LOOK EXACTLY LIKE THE LEAVES OF PLANTS.

DESERT LOCUST

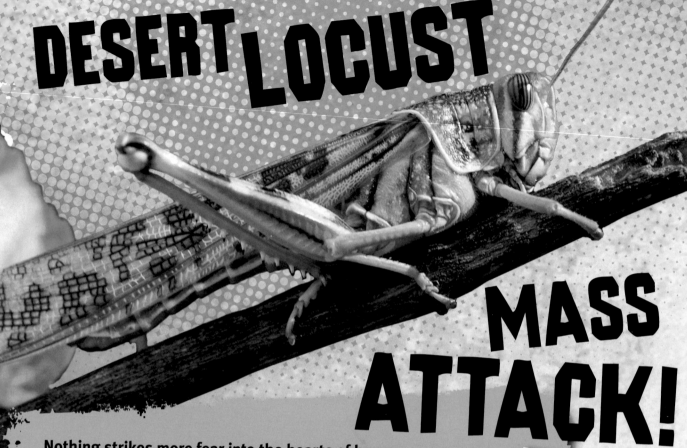

MASS ATTACK!

Nothing strikes more fear into the hearts of hungry people than a plague of desert locusts. These six-legged supervillains usually live alone but may gather in gigantic swarms, devastating crops across millions of square kilometres. Desert locusts contribute to the problems of famine and starvation in developing countries, particularly in Africa, by eating the crops that people rely on for food.

The desert locust is one of about 15 species of locust. These large insects spend most of their time alone, living in the deserts of Africa, the Middle East and eastern parts of Asia. Unlike many insects, which undergo complete metamorphosis from an egg to a larva and then to the adult insect, locusts undergo incomplete metamorphosis. The young locusts, called nymphs, hatch as miniature versions of the adult insects and go through six stages of development. At each stage, the locust sheds its hard outer skin, called an exoskeleton, and grows into a new skin underneath.

CRITTER STATS!

Size: Up to 7.5 cm long
Number of species: 1
Habitat: Deserts of Africa, Asia and the Middle East

THE HUMAN FACTOR

IN MANY COUNTRIES AROUND THE WORLD, PEOPLE RELY ON LOCUSTS AS A SOURCE OF FOOD. THE LOCUSTS ARE AN IMPORTANT SOURCE OF PROTEIN WHEN OTHER FOODS, PARTICULARLY PLANT CROPS, ARE IN SHORT SUPPLY – ALL THANKS TO THE HUNGRY LOCUST PESTS!

SUPER NATURAL POWER!

The solitary life of the desert locusts soon changes when it rains. This prompts the female to lay her eggs in the sandy desert soil. The rain spurs new plant growth, so there is food and shelter available for the nymphs when they hatch. **More and more locusts swarm around the plants**, which triggers changes in the insects' metabolism. First, they change colour and their bodies become shorter. Then **they release a chemical pheromone** that enhances the swarming behaviour.

PLAGUE PROPORTIONS

Very quickly, a swarm of locusts can **grow to epic proportions**. A single swarm can cover thousands of square kilometres, with **between 40 and 80 million locusts** in each square kilometre. The hungry swarm munches its way through any plants it meets – including important crops. **The last major plague occurred in 2004** in West Africa. Farmers in more than 20 countries lost up to US$2.5 billion worth of crops.

AWESOME!

A DESERT LOCUST CAN EAT ITS BODYWEIGHT IN PLANTS EVERY DAY, SO A SWARM OF HUNGRY LOCUSTS CAN HAVE DEVASTATING CONSEQUENCES ACROSS WIDE AREAS OF FARMLAND.

WOW!

A SWARM OF DESERT LOCUSTS CAN FLY UP TO 200 KILOMETRES EVERY DAY.

MEANWHILE, AT THE MOVIES...

SUPERHERO STYLE

MANY COMIC BOOK CHARACTERS JOIN FORCES TO FIGHT THEIR ENEMIES, WHILE ONE ANIMATED VILLAIN HAS EVEN APPEARED AS A GIANT LOCUST.

AVENGERS

A CRACK TEAM OF MARVEL COMIC SUPERHEROES THAT ORIGINALLY INCLUDED IRON MAN, ANT-MAN, WASP, THOR AND HULK. CAPTAIN AMERICA JOINED THE AVENGERS AFTER THE TEAM FREED HIM FROM A BLOCK OF ICE.

ZORAK

A GIANT LOCUST (OR PRAYING MANTIS, DEPENDING ON THE EPISODE) NAMED ZORAK APPEARED AS AN ADVERSARY TO SPACE GHOST IN THE 1990S CARTOON 'SPACE GHOST COAST TO COAST'.

THE SUPER-STRONG DUNG BEETLE

Can you imagine making your home in a pile of animal dung? One group of insects does exactly that – the aptly named dung beetles, which use their super sense of smell to home in on the nearest pile of animal droppings. This may seem gross, but these six-legged superheroes do a vital job, helping to clean the soil and recycle valuable nutrients.

There are many **thousands of different dung beetles** that live in most of the world's habitats, from deserts and farms to grasslands and forests. In fact, the only place where dung beetles cannot survive is in the frozen wasteland of Antarctica. These hardy beetles are so successful because they feed on a readily available food source that most other animals choose to ignore – **animal poo.**

CRITTER STATS!

Size: From 1mm to 6cm
Number of species: 30,000
Habitat: Most habitats

MEANWHILE, AT THE MOVIES...

SUPERHERO STYLE

WELL-KNOWN COMIC BOOK CHARACTERS AND ACTION HEROES WITH BEETLE-LIKE SUPERPOWERS INCLUDE:

SCARAB THE SECRET IDENTITY OF EGYPTOLOGIST PETER WARD, WHO TRANSFORMED INTO A SUPER-POWERFUL SCARAB (DUNG) BEETLE WHEN HE RUBBED HIS MAGIC SCARAB RING. (THE ANCIENT EGYPTIANS WORSHIPPED DUNG BEETLES CALLED SCARABS.)

SILVER SCARAB ANOTHER BEETLE-BASED COMIC-BOOK CHARACTER WITH SUPERHUMAN STRENGTH AND THE ABILITY TO FLY IN OUTER SPACE.

SUPER NATURAL POWER!

Dung beetles use their **amazing sense of smell** to detect their next meal. Many species fly forwards and backwards across the wind until they pick up the scent of a pile of dung. Then they move upwind to locate their target.

Different dung beetles have different feeding strategies. Some **mould the animal dung into huge balls** and roll them around as a mobile food store. Others store animal droppings in underground 'larders'. A few species actually lay their eggs in the dung, and the larvae deplete the nutrients in the dung as they grow into adult beetles. **A freshly laid pile of dung** will attract numerous dung beetles in a matter of minutes.

AWESOME!

SCIENTISTS WORKING IN KRUGER NATIONAL PARK IN SOUTH AFRICA ONCE COUNTED 16,00 DUNG BEETLES IN A SINGLE PILE OF ELEPHANT POO!.

WOW!

A SINGLE DUNG BEETLE CAN ROLL A BALL OF DUNG MANY TIMES ITS OWN WEIGHT.

BEETLE DRIVE

Along with their extrasensory scent detection, scientists think that dung beetles have an even more amazing superpower. In a recent study, scientists showed dung beetles might **use stars as a guide to help them roll balls of animal waste** along the ground. The study suggested that by following stars in the night sky, dung beetles roll their prized food source in a straight line away from the pile of animal dung, where other dung beetles might be waiting to steal it.

THE EARTHWORM HAS AN AMAZING ABILITY TO REGENERATE SECTIONS OF ITS SEGMENTED BODY.

THE BIONIC EARTHWORM

CRITTER STATS!

Size: Up to 35 cm long
Number of species: 1
Habitat: Soil

The common earthworm is an invertebrate – an animal without a backbone. In fact, the earthworm is nothing more than a long segmented tube with a head at one end and a tail at the other. Earthworms burrow through the soil, feeding on dead and living plant and animal material buried in the ground. The most amazing thing about these simple creatures is their bionic ability to regenerate body segments.

The earthworm's body consists of ring-like segments covered with tiny hairs, which help the worm grip as they burrow under the ground. By squirming its body through the mud, **earthworms help to mix up and aerate the soil** and provide drainage channels for water running through the ground. **Earthworms are also natural recyclers.** They help clean up the soil by feeding on the rotting remains of plants and animals.

THE HUMAN FACTOR

EARTHWORMS ARE IMPORTANT TO PEOPLE FOR MANY DIFFERENT REASONS. NOT ONLY DO THEY MAINTAIN THE QUALITY OF THE SOIL, WE USE THEM IN A PRACTICE CALLED VERMICULTURE. THIS IS WHEN EARTHWORMS ARE USED IN COMPOST HEAPS TO DECOMPOSE HUMAN FOOD WASTE. IN SOME CULTURES, SUCH AS THE MAORI OF NEW ZEALAND, PEOPLE EAT EARTHWORMS – LOCALLY CALLED NOKE – AS A DELICACY. ANYONE FANCY WORM SPAGHETTI?

SUPER NATURAL POWER!

If you were cruel enough to cut a common earthworm in half, you might be surprised to find out that the head end develops into a new fully grown worm. **The bionic power of the earthworm** is a response to predators such as garden birds, moles, snakes and toads, which rely on the worms as an important food source. The first stage in this regeneration is the healing of the wound. Cells then start to grow beneath the wound, forming **a structure called a blastema**. Gradually, the mass of cells in the blastema lengthens and grows into a new tail end.

MEANWHILE, AT THE MOVIES...
SUPERHERO STYLE

COMIC-BOOK CHARACTERS AND ACTION HEROES AND VILLAINS WITH REGENERATING SUPERPOWERS INCLUDE:

THE DOCTOR THE CENTRAL CHARACTER FROM THE POPULAR BBC TELEVISION SERIES 'DOCTOR WHO' CAN REGENERATE FROM BEING SEVERELY WOUNDED.

WOLVERINE THIS MARVEL COMICS SUPERHERO HAS STAYED ALIVE DESPITE BEING SHOT MANY TIMES THANKS TO ENHANCED REGENERATIVE HEALING.

FEEDING FRENZY

Earthworms feed as they burrow through the soil. This forces mud through the earthworm's gut – a long, straight tube that runs from the mouth to the worm's bottom. The earthworm absorbs any food matter and the waste passes out through the worm's rear end and into the soil. You can see the earthworm's poo as worm casts on the surface of the soil.

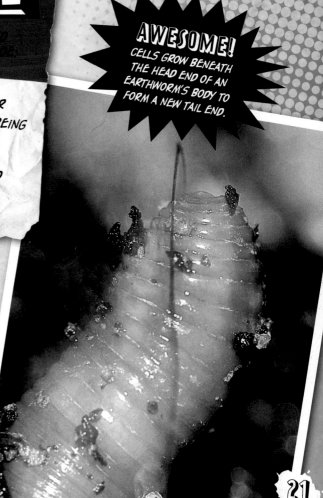

AWESOME! CELLS GROW BENEATH THE HEAD END OF AN EARTHWORM'S BODY TO FORM A NEW TAIL END.

THE SUPER-STINGING FIRE ANT

There are more than 285 different fire ant species that live in most places around the world. These small insects have many different common names, including ginger ants, red ants and tropical red ants. Fire ants inject venom using a stinger instead of spraying acid over attackers like many other ant species.

Fire ants are typical insects, with three distinct body segments – the head, thorax and abdomen – a pair of antennae on the head and three pairs of legs on each body segment. **These ants live in large groups called colonies.** They build nests in the soil, which are usually hidden underneath logs or rocks. In open spaces, the ants often build their nest and cover it with a large mound of soil.

SUPER NATURAL POWER!

Most ants attack their enemies by biting them and then **spraying a corrosive chemical** called formic acid over the bite wound. Fire ants also bite but only to grasp on to their opponent. Once it has got a good grip, **the ant then injects venom** using a stinger in its tail. The venom is potent enough to kill most prey animals and is an effective weapon against most predators.

When people are stung by fire ants they experience a **strong burning sensation.** In most cases, the area of the sting swells into a bump for a few days and then disappears. In a few serious cases, people can have an allergic reaction to the sting, which can be **fatal without emergency treatment.**

ANT JOBS

Different ants have different roles within the colony. All colonies contain at least one queen ant. The queen pairs up with male ants called drones, which die immediately after mating. The queen then lays her eggs – **up to 3,500 eggs every day.** The soldier ants guard all the other ants in the colony. They have bigger jaws, called mandibles, to bite their enemies. The workers do all the other jobs in the colony, such as cleaning, foraging for food and caring for the larvae.

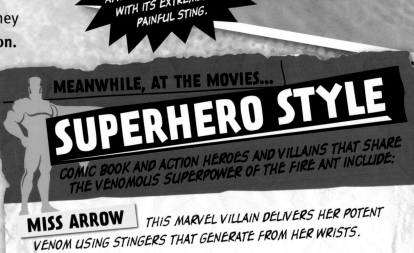

AWESOME!
A FIRE ANT PREPARES TO ATTACK ITS HUMAN VICTIM WITH ITS EXTREMEMLY PAINFUL STING.

MEANWHILE, AT THE MOVIES...

SUPERHERO STYLE

COMIC BOOK AND ACTION HEROES AND VILLAINS THAT SHARE THE VENOMOUS SUPERPOWER OF THE FIRE ANT INCLUDE:

MISS ARROW THIS MARVEL VILLAIN DELIVERS HER POTENT VENOM USING STINGERS THAT GENERATE FROM HER WRISTS.

THE JOKER BATMAN'S ARCH-ENEMY SOMETIMES USES A TOXIC CHEMICAL COCKTAIL CALLED JOKER VENOM TO IMMOBILIZE HIS OPPONENTS.

WOW!
QUEEN ANTS ARE THE BIGGEST AND MOST IMPORTANT MEMBERS OF A FIRE ANT COLONY.

THE HIGH-JUMPING BLOOD-SUCKING FLEA

CRITTER STATS!

Size: Up to 3.5 mm

Number of species: 2000

Habitat: Parasitic

Fleas are wingless insects that live on the bodies of host animals such as birds and mammals. These small parasites have sharp piercing mouthparts to break through the skin of their hosts and drink up their blood. One of the flea's most amazing superpowers is its ability to jump great distances.

There are more than 2,000 different flea species that live on the bodies of a number of different **warm-blooded hosts**, from cats and chickens to rats, dogs and even people.

THE HUMAN FACTOR

IN MEDIEVAL EUROPE, FLEAS LIVING ON RATS SPREAD ONE OF THE DEADLIEST DISEASES IN HUMAN HISTORY - BUBONIC PLAGUE, ALSO KNOWN AS THE BLACK DEATH. FLEAS ARE RESPONSIBLE FOR SPREADING MANY OTHER HUMAN DISEASES, INCLUDING CAT-SCRATCH DISEASE AND TAPEWORM INFECTIONS.

WOW!
THE RED MARK ON THE CAT'S SKIN SHOWS THAT IT HAS BEEN BITTEN BY A FLEA.

SUPER NATURAL POWER!

Most fleas are small insects, measuring no more than 3.5 mm in length. But they can jump up to 18 cm directly upwards and more than 30 cm across – from a standstill!

The amazing jumping ability of the flea is not due to muscle power. Instead, these insects use the energy stored in a protein called resilin, which is found in the flea's long back legs. This substance provides the spring action to get the flea airborne. The flea then homes in on the body heat and vibrations of its host.

FANTASTIC FLEAS

Fleas have a number of adaptations to life as parasitic insects. For a start, they have flattened bodies, which means they can move easily through the fur or feathers that cover the bodies of their hosts. The flea's body is also hard, shiny and **covered with backward-pointing hairs** and spines, which also help the fleas move about on their hosts. The body of the flea is also tough – **it is almost impossible to squash a flea** with your fingers. This is probably another adaptation to life as a parasite, preventing the host from **scratching or crushing the flea to kill it.**

AWESOME!
THE FLEA IS ONE OF THE BEST JUMPERS OF THE ANIMAL KINGDOM, RELATIVE TO ITS BODY SIZE. IT IS SHOWN HERE AS SEEN UNDER AN ELECTRON MICROSCOPE.

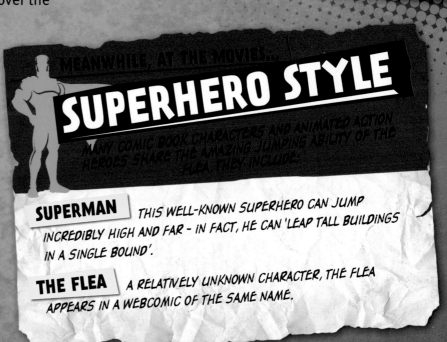

MEANWHILE, AT THE MOVIES...

SUPERHERO STYLE

MANY COMIC BOOK CHARACTERS AND ANIMATED ACTION HEROES SHARE THE AMAZING JUMPING ABILITY OF THE FLEA. THEY INCLUDE:

SUPERMAN THIS WELL-KNOWN SUPERHERO CAN JUMP INCREDIBLY HIGH AND FAR – IN FACT, HE CAN 'LEAP TALL BUILDINGS IN A SINGLE BOUND'.

THE FLEA A RELATIVELY UNKNOWN CHARACTER, THE FLEA APPEARS IN A WEBCOMIC OF THE SAME NAME.

THE FUNGUS GNAT
GLOW WORM

These glow worms are the larvae of one of four species of fungus gnats – tiny, short-lived flies that live in caves and sheltered forests of Australia and New Zealand. The tiny flies belong to the group (genus) Arachnocampa, which means 'spider worm'.

Fungus gnats spend most of their lives as larvae. After mating with the male, the female fungus gnat lays her eggs in two or three clumps of 40 to 50 eggs. The larvae hatch about 20 days later, and they spin a silk nest on a cave roof or overhanging branch. The larvae then spin up to 70 silky threads and hang them from the bottom of the nest. Each thread holds **sticky blobs of mucus to snare passing prey** – anything from caddis flies and mayflies to moths and mosquitoes. The sticky mucus blobs contain venom to **paralyse and subdue the prey** to make it easier to eat.

WOW!

THE GLOW WORMS MIMIC SPIDERS BY HANGING STICKY SILK THREADS FROM THE ROOF OF A CAVE, USING THEM TO CATCH PREY.

CRITTER STATS!

Size: Up to 3 cm
Number of species: 4
Habitat: Caves and sheltered forests

SUPER NATURAL POWER!

The fungus gnat larva is often called a glow worm because it glows in the dark. Since the female lays her eggs in clumps, there can be hundreds of glowing larvae on the cave roof, and they look like stars in the sky at night. This glowing light show lures prey towards the sticky threads below the nests. When a fly or other unfortunate victim hits the sticky snare, it becomes trapped. The larva then slowly pulls the victim up on its thread to feed.

LETHAL LIGHT LURE

An amazing process called bioluminescence gives the fungus gnat its glow. The larva produces a chemical called luciferin, which is stored in the gnat larva's abdomen. This substance reacts with an enzyme and oxygen to glow brightly. The glow dims after the larvae have eaten, so the hungriest larvae glow the brightest.

AWESOME!

THE GLOWING LIGHT SHOW LURES PREY TOWARDS THE STICKY THREADS BELOW THE NESTS.

LIFE CYCLE

The fungus gnats live as larvae for up to 12 months. Then, they pupate, which means they form a cocoon and transform into the adult gnats. The females continue to glow, which attracts the males to mate with them. After mating, the female lays her eggs and the life cycle continues.

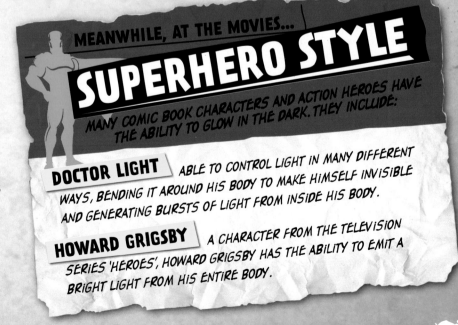

MEANWHILE, AT THE MOVIES...

SUPERHERO STYLE

MANY COMIC BOOK CHARACTERS AND ACTION HEROES HAVE THE ABILITY TO GLOW IN THE DARK. THEY INCLUDE:

DOCTOR LIGHT ABLE TO CONTROL LIGHT IN MANY DIFFERENT WAYS, BENDING IT AROUND HIS BODY TO MAKE HIMSELF INVISIBLE AND GENERATING BURSTS OF LIGHT FROM INSIDE HIS BODY.

HOWARD GRIGSBY A CHARACTER FROM THE TELEVISION SERIES 'HEROES', HOWARD GRIGSBY HAS THE ABILITY TO EMIT A BRIGHT LIGHT FROM HIS ENTIRE BODY.

THE GIANT GOLIATH
BIRD-EATING SPIDER

The goliath bird-eating spider is a monster-sized tarantula with a huge appetite to match its gigantic size. This deadly arachnid takes its name from the eyewitness reports of 19th century English explorers, who saw them feasting on hummingbirds in the rainforests of South America.

One of the world's biggest arachnids, no other spider comes near to matching the goliath bird-eating spider's huge body mass. Only one other species – the giant huntsman spider – has a bigger leg span.

Although the goliath bird-eating spider is definitely big enough to eat a bird, this hardly ever happens. These spiders live underground in burrows and seldom chance upon bird prey other than chicks that have fallen out of their nests near the entrance to their burrows.

WOW!

THE SHARP FANGS AND HAIRY BODY OF THE GOLIATH BIRD-EATING SPIDER MAKE IT A FORMIDABLE FOE.

CRITTER STATS!

Size: Leg span of 30cm
Number of species: 1
Habitat: South American rainforests

SUPER NATURAL POWER!

The goliath bird-eating spider is armed with a deadly arsenal. The spider's fangs (see right) are as long and as sharp as a cat's claws and can **puncture through flesh with ease.** These spiders are ambush predators and sit at the entrance to their burrows, waiting for passing prey. When a suitably sized animal passes by, the spider darts forward and **injects venom into the body of its victim.** The venom paralyses the helpless prey, leaving the spider free to feed.

HAIR RAISING!

Despite its long, sharp fangs, the goliath bird-eating spider will only bite as a last resort. The body of **this spider is extraordinarily hairy** and provides the arachnid with a clever form of defence. When threatened, most spiders will simply retreat to the safety of their burrows and wait for the danger to pass. But the goliath bird-eating spider also uses its legs to kick hairs on its abdomen towards an attacker. The goliath bird-eating spider rubs its legs together, **creating a hissing sound** to ward off unwanted attention. The hairs are covered with tiny spines and are irritating if they come into contact with the skin, eyes or mouth.

MEANWHILE, AT THE MOVIES...

SUPERHERO STYLE

WELL-KNOWN COMIC BOOK CHARACTERS AND ACTION HEROES WITH SIMILAR SPIDER-LIKE WEAPONRY INCLUDE:

SPIDER-MAN
THE ALTER-EGO OF PETER PARKER, WHO WAS BITTEN BY A RADIOACTIVE SPIDER WHEN HE WAS A TEENAGER, WHICH GAVE HIM HIS AMAZING ARACHNID POWERS.

BLACK WIDOW
THE ARCH-ENEMY OF IRON MAN, WHO LATER PUT HER AMAZING SPIDER-LIKE AGILITY TO GOOD USE IN THE FIGHT AGAINST EVIL SUPERPOWERS.

AWESOME!
AS NOCTURNAL CREATURES THESE SPIDERS ARE ACTIVE AT NIGHT, SPENDING THE DAY IN DAMP, DARK BURROWS.

THE SUPER-STRONG

HERCULES BEETLE

The Hercules beetle is one of six species of rhinoceros beetles, which live in the tropical rainforests of Central and South America. Named after the super-strong hero of Greek legend, the Hercules beetle is, for its size, one of the world's strongest animals.

The biggest of the six rhinoceros beetles, the Hercules beetle is **one of the largest beetles in the world.** Only the colossal titan beetle, which also lives in the rainforests of South America, is bigger. The long 'rhino' horns of the Hercules beetle make up most of its length. Only male beetles have the giant horns. The female beetles have bigger bodies but, without the long horns, are always shorter than the males.

RHINOCEROS BEETLES TAKE THEIR NAME FROM THEIR LONG HORNS, WHICH LOOK LIKE THE HORN OF A RHINO.

SUPER NATURAL POWER!

The Hercules beetle takes its common name from the Greek hero Hercules, who was noted for his amazing strength and fearless nature. The Hercules beetle certainly lives up to its name. While a single beetle weighs in at about 85g, it can lift **up to 850 times its own body weight** – that's the same as an adult human lifting ten African elephants!

FEMALE HERCULES BEETLES HAVE LARGER BODIES THAN THE MALES.

FANCY THAT!

The horns of the male beetles may look like formidable weapons, but they are rarely used for this purpose. In fact, male beetles use their long horns to **show off their strength and fitness** to the females. Males with longer horns will usually attract more females. On rare occasions, two males will fight for the affection of the female. The winner is the male that **flips his rival onto his back**.

MEANWHILE, AT THE MOVIES...

SUPERHERO STYLE

SEVERAL COMIC BOOK CHARACTERS AND ACTION HEROES ARE NOTED FOR THEIR AMAZING STRENGTH. THEY INCLUDE:

SUPERMAN
THIS FAMOUS SUPERHERO IS THE MOST POWERFUL OF ALL LIVING THINGS AND HAS SHOWN SEVERAL SUPERHUMAN FEATS OF STRENGTH. SUPERMAN CAN LIFT MORE THAN ONE MILLION TONNES WITH EASE.

THE INCREDIBLE HULK
ONE OF THE STRONGEST SUPERHEROES OF ALL, HULK GETS EVEN STRONGER THE ANGRIER HE BECOMES.

AWESOME!

DESPITE THEIR FEARSOME APPEARANCE, HERCULES BEETLES ARE HERBIVORES, FEEDING ON RIPE AND DECAYING FRUIT.

THE HIMALAYAN 'HIGH' JUMPING SPIDER

CRITTER STATS!

Size: Around 15 mm
Number of species: 1
Habitat: High mountains

The Himalayan jumping spider is a tiny acrobatic arachnid that literally lives on top of the world – high on the slopes of the world's tallest mountain, Mount Everest. In fact, this hardy jumping spider manages to survive at more than 6,700 metres above sea level, making it one of the highest-known living animals on Earth!

The scientific species name of the Himalayan jumping spider is *omnisuperstes*, which means 'standing above everything'. These brave spiders are certainly one of the few animals that can survive at such a high altitude. They brave the **wild winds and freezing mountain temperatures** by hiding in rock crevices.

THE HIMALAYAN JUMPING SPIDER LIVES ON TOP OF THE WORLD, ON THE SLOPES OF MOUNT EVEREST.

SUPER NATURAL POWER!

Since there are no other living animals that make their home high in mountains, Himalayan jumping spiders feed on stray insects and other debris that blow up from the lower slopes. Like all jumping spiders, this high-altitude arachnid does not spin a web to trap passing insects. Instead, it spins a single silk thread and **uses it as a safety cord** to anchor its body to a rock or other solid object.

SPRING ACTION

When an insect floats past in the wind, **the spider springs into action**. It uses a rapid pulse of hydraulic pressure in its back legs to pounce on passing insects. In this way, **the jumping spider can leap incredible distances** – many times its own body size. If the spider misses its prey, it simply pulls itself back along the safety cord (seen at the top right of this picture) and waits for another opportunity to feed.

AWESOME!

THERE ARE MORE THAN 5,000 SPECIES OF JUMPING SPIDER. THEY ALL HUNT FOR PREY USING THEIR FANTASTIC EYESIGHT AND AMAZING JUMPING ABILITY.

MEANWHILE, AT THE MOVIES...

SUPERHERO STYLE

COMIC BOOK CHARACTERS AND ACTION HEROES WHO DEMONSTRATE AN AMAZING JUMPING ABILITY INCLUDE:

SPIDER-MAN

SPIDER-MAN IS FAMOUS FOR HIS SUPERHUMAN LEAPING SKILLS AND CAN LEAP BETWEEN BUILDINGS WITH EASE, USING WEBLINES TO HELP HIM.

SUPERMAN

SUPERMAN WAS ONE OF THE FIRST SUPERHEROES TO USE ENHANCED JUMPING AND WAS 'ABLE TO LEAP TALL BUILDINGS IN A SINGLE BOUND'.

SAFETY CORD

THE ANTI-GRAVITY SUPER-SENSORY HOUSEFLY

The common housefly is the fly you will most often find flying around inside your home, buzzing around and generally causing a nuisance. These pesky pests have such a bad reputation because they spread so many diseases. Houseflies have an amazing array of supernatural senses and can even defy gravity by walking upside down!

Houseflies spend a lot of time crawling over **animal poo, rubbish and rotting flesh.** After these pests feed and lay their eggs on this putrid mess, they fly into our homes and spread the germs all over our food and belongings. Yuk! These are the same germs that cause a number of **potentially deadly diseases,** including cholera, tuberculosis and typhoid fever.

CRITTER STATS!

Size: 2 cm long
Number of species: 1
Habitat: Worldwide

THE HUMAN FACTOR

HOUSEFLIES MAY HAVE A NUMBER OF DISGUSTING HABITS, BUT THEY ARE ALSO HELPFUL TO PEOPLE AND OTHER ANIMALS. FIRST, HOUSEFLIES AND THEIR LARVAE ALSO PROVIDE FOOD FOR MANY DIFFERENT CREATURES. THE FLIES ALSO HELP RECYCLE NUTRIENTS AND CLEAN UP THE ENVIRONMENT BY BREAKING DOWN WASTE MATERIAL.

SUPER NATURAL POWER!

If you have ever tried to swat a housefly, you will know how frustrating it can be. They seem to second-guess every swipe and you end up missing more times than scoring a hit. **Houseflies have an array of sharp senses** – primarily to avoid the many predators that want to eat them. First, houseflies have excellent all-round vision, with two large compound eyes containing 6,000 individual lenses each. They also have three extra simple eyes, which act like a compass and tell the fly which way is up.

FANTASTIC FEET

Houseflies also have fantastic senses of smell and taste. They smell using their antennae and taste with their long tongue, called a proboscis. In addition, houseflies can taste food with their feet! These super-sensitive feet also provide the housefly with its **amazing anti-gravity crawling abilities**. Each footpad has tiny claws and moist suction cups called pulvilli, which allow the fly to grip onto slippery glass surfaces and even crawl upside down.

FEEDING FRENZY

If you think the housefly's choice of food is gross, then you will definitely not like its table manners! The housefly cannot bite or chew so they cannot eat solid food. Instead, it vomits a mixture of saliva and digestive juices over its meal before sucking up the liquid goo.

WOW!
A HOUSEFLY'S FEET ARE TEN MILLION TIMES MORE SENSITIVE THAN THE HUMAN TONGUE.

MEANWHILE, AT THE MOVIES...

SUPERHERO STYLE

COMIC BOOK CHARACTERS AND ACTION HEROES WITH AN AWESOME ANTI-GRAVITY CLIMBING ABILITY INCLUDE:

NIGHTCRAWLER THIS SUPERHERO CAN SCALE SHEER SURFACES WITH EASE USING SUCTION CUPS ATTACHED TO HIS HANDS AND FEET.

SPIDER-MAN SPIDER-MAN IS ONE OF THE MOST FAMOUS SUPERHEROES WHO USES HIS WALL-CRAWLING ABILITY TO STICK TO SEEMINGLY IMPOSSIBLE SURFACES SUCH AS GLASS.

THE BOILING JAPENESE HONEYBEE

CRITTER STATS!

Size: 15 mm long

Number of species: 1

Habitat: Forests, grasslands and urban areas

THE HUMAN FACTOR

BEEKEEPERS IN JAPAN HAVE DOMESTICATED JAPANESE HONEYBEES TO HARVEST HONEY AND OTHER PRODUCTS OF THE HIVE, SUCH AS BEESWAX AND ROYAL JELLY. THE PRACTICE OF BEEKEEPING IS KNOWN AS APICULTURE AND DATES BACK TO THE TIME OF THE ANCIENT EGYPTIANS.

The Japanese honeybee is the Asian relative of the European honeybee. These insects range over much of southern and Southeast Asia, where they nest in enclosed spaces such as hollow tree trunks. Japanese honeybees will do almost anything to protect the hive – including cooking its enemies alive!

Japanese honeybees are social insects that live in groups called colonies. **A colony may contain up to 40,000 bees.** Every bee a specific job, from the egg-laying queen to the industrious workers. The queen uses **chemicals called pheromones** to signal to other members of the colony. This tells the workers that she is fertile. The workers communicate to each other using complex 'dances'. In this way, they communicate the location of nearby sources of food (plant nectar) and water.

SUPER NATURAL POWER!

The Asian giant hornet (right) is the main predator of the Japanese honeybee. The hornets are deadly killers – 30 to 40 can wipe out an entire colony of bees in a few hours, using their massive mandibles (jaws) to **tear the bees and their larvae apart**. However, the bees sometimes fight back...

The hornets usually send out a scout to search for honeybee hives. When it does, the hornet scout crawls inside and **sprays the bees with a pheromone**. This acts as a signal to other hornets to home in on the hive. But the hornet is in for a nasty surprise. Hundreds of bees soon swarm around the hornet scout and start to rub their wings together. This raises the temperature inside the hive to 47°C (117°F), and **the hornet is slowly cooked alive**.

MEANWHILE, AT THE MOVIES...
SUPERHERO STYLE

SEVERAL COMIC BOOK CHARACTERS AND ACTION HEROES HARNESS THE POWER OF HEAT AS A SUPERPOWER. THEY INCLUDE:

HUMAN TORCH THIS FIERY SUPERHERO HAS THE ABILITY TO ENVELOP HIS BODY WITH SUPERHOT PLASMA AND SHOOT FIREBALLS AT HIS ENEMIES.

MAGMA THIS FEMALE SUPERHERO HARNESSES THE NATURAL HEAT FROM EARTH'S CORE TO FIGHT HER RIVALS.

WOW!
A HEATED MOUND OF HONEYBEES SWAMPS ITS WOULD-BE ATTACKERS..

AWESOME!
THE SWARM DEPARTS, LEAVING THE BODIES OF THE DEAD HORNETS BEHIND.

THE DEADLY MOSQUITO

Mosquitoes live in most parts of the world, except Antarctica. These tiny flies may look harmless, but they are one of the most dangerous animals on Earth. Female mosquitoes are pests with a thirst for blood. When they feed on human blood, some species pass on parasites that cause the deadly disease malaria.

There are more than 3,000 different mosquito species, but only a few carry the parasites that spread malaria. These mosquitoes live in tropical parts of the world, including Africa, Asia and Central and South America. Mosquitoes are **equipped with a range of super-senses** to home in on their next meal.

CRITTER STATS!

Size: Up to 16 mm
Number of species: More than 3,000
Habitat: Worldwide

THE HUMAN FACTOR

MALARIA IS THE ONE OF THE WORLD'S DEADLIEST DISEASES. EVERY YEAR, HUNDREDS OF MILLIONS OF PEOPLE ARE INFECTED WITH MALARIA PARASITES, AND MILLIONS MORE DIE. ONE OF THE BEST WAYS TO STOP THE SPREAD OF MALARIA IS BY SLEEPING UNDER A MOSQUITO NET.

AWESOME!

MOSQUITOES USE THEIR LARGE COMPOUND EYES TO TRACK THE MOVEMENTS OF THEIR PREY.

SUPER NATURAL POWER!

WOW! A MOSQUITO USES ITS LONG PROBOSCIS TO PIERCE HUMAN SKIN.

Mosquitoes rely on **chemical, visual and thermal clues** to sense their prey. The mosquito's antennae are sensitive to chemicals such as carbon monoxide and lactic acid, which are produced as by-products of our normal breathing. Mosquitoes also have excellent eyesight and see in colour, so they can easily spot a tourist in bright shorts and a tee shirt!

Chemicals in our sweat also attract mosquitoes, and sweating is hard to avoid in hot, tropical countries. In addition, mosquitoes home in on the body heat of their prey – so warm-blooded humans are fairly easy for mosquitoes to find.

PASSING ON PARASITES

Female mosquitoes pass on the parasites that cause malaria when they feed on human blood. They use their long proboscis to penetrate the skin and reach into the blood vessels below. To prevent the blood from clotting, the mosquitoes **inject saliva into the wound**. This saliva contains the malaria parasites, which then pass into the bloodstream and cause the disease.

MEANWHILE, AT THE MOVIES...

SUPERHERO STYLE

COMIC-BOOK CHARACTERS AND SUPERHEROES WHO RELY ON BLOOD TO GIVE THEM SUPERNATURAL POWERS INCLUDE:

BLADE THIS MARVEL COMICS SUPERHERO HAS MANY SUPERHUMAN ABILITIES, SUCH AS STRENGTH, STAMINA, SPEED AND AGILITY – AS WELL AS AN INSATIABLE APPETITE FOR BLOOD!

DRACULA PERHAPS THE WORLD'S MOST FAMOUS VAMPIRE, COUNT DRACULA IS THE CENTRAL CHARACTER IN THE GOTHIC HORROR NOVEL BY IRISH WRITER BRAM STOKER.

AWESOME! ITS BODY RED WITH BLOOD, A MOSQUITO FEEDS ON ITS HUMAN PREY.

THE ARMOURED MOTH BUTTERFLY CATERPILLAR

The caterpillar of the moth butterfly *Liphyra brassolis* lives in the tropical rainforests of southern and Southeast Asia and Australia. The moth butterfly is fairly unremarkable as an adult, but the caterpillar has built a reputation as a bit of brute! This carnivorous caterpillar has an unusual appetite for weaver ants.

The female moth butterfly lays her eggs on the underside of branches, carefully selecting trees that are home to colonies of weaver ants. The ants live in nests built from leaves, which are held together using **sticky strands of silk**. One tree may contain several ant nests, and each nest may be home to hundreds of worker ants, a queen, and the ant grubs. After about three weeks, the moth butterfly egg hatches. The caterpillar then makes its home in an ant nest, **attacking and feasting on the hundreds of larvae inside.**

WEAVER ANTS WORK TOGETHER TO BUILD A NEST, BUT WILL IT BE UNDER THREAT FROM THE MOTH BUTTERFLY CATERPILLAR?

CRITTER STATS!

Size: About 3 cm
Number of species: 1
Habitat: Rainforests

SUPER NATURAL POWER!

Ants are not the most welcome of hosts – they bite and consume most intruders – **but the moth butterfly caterpillar thrives inside the nest**. These gatecrashers survive because they have thick, tough skin – the ants cannot bite through this **heavy suit of armour**. The ants even try to flip the caterpillar onto its back to attack the softer underside, but the caterpillar has strong, sucker-like feet to stick it firmly in place.

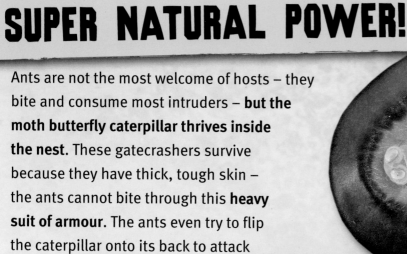

ANT ATTACK!

So the helpless ants can only watch in horror as the moth butterfly caterpillar starts to attack the ant grubs. The caterpillar drags them under its protective shield, sucks out the juices and discards the empty shell before moving on to its next victim. A hungry caterpillar can **devour as many as ten grubs every hour**.

MEANWHILE, AT THE MOVIES...

SUPERHERO STYLE

COMIC BOOK CHARACTERS AND ACTION HEROES AND VILLAINS WHO USE DEFENSIVE BODY ARMOUR INCLUDE:

IRON MAN
WEARS A POWERED SUIT OF ARMOUR THAT GIVES HIM SUPERHUMAN STRENGTH AND AGILITY, AS WELL AS THE ABILITY TO FLY.

THE THING
THE BODY OF THIS MARVEL SUPERHERO IS COVERED WITH AN ORANGE, FLEXIBLE, ROCK-LIKE HIDE, WHICH PROTECTS HIM FROM BULLETS, BOMBS AND OTHER WEAPONS.

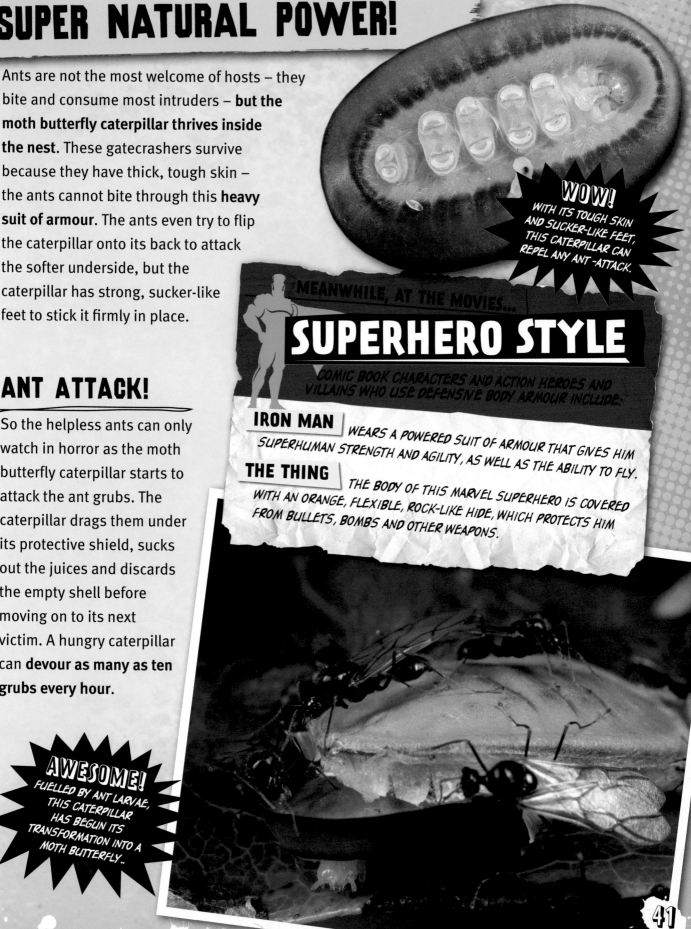

AWESOME!
FUELLED BY ANT LARVAE, THIS CATERPILLAR HAS BEGUN ITS TRANSFORMATION INTO A MOTH BUTTERFLY...

THE TRANSPARENT SNAIL

The transparent snail is a miniature mollusc that lives in central and Western Europe, creeping across alpine meadows and woodlands in search of plant food. The most amazing thing about these tiny snails is their see-through shells, which give them an air of invisibility.

Like most land snails, the transparent snail has a **huge appetite for plants.** It eats the flowers, fruits, leaves and succulent tree bark, as well as the rotting remains of plant parts. Snails have a hard, rough structure called a radula inside their mouths. The radula is like a bit like a nail file, with **rows of tiny teeth** that scrape and grind up plant food. Occasionally, the transparent snail will eat dead earthworms and horse manure.

WOW!

DUE TO THEIR APPEARANCE, TRANSPARENT SNAILS ARE OFTEN ALSO KNOWN AS GLASS SNAILS.

CRITTER STATS!

Size: Up to 6 mm
Number of species: 1
Habitat: Moist, shady places

SUPER NATURAL POWER!

Most snails are born with soft, transparent shells. As they develop into adults, the shells usually harden and form their final colour (like the snail in the picture at the top of this page). But the **paper-thin shell** of the transparent snail (see below) stays see-through for its whole life, giving the snail a **ghostly, invisible appearance**.

THE HUMAN FACTOR

SNAILS ARE THE NUMBER ONE ENEMY OF FARMERS AND GARDENERS. THESE PESKY PESTS CAUSE A LOT OF DAMAGE IN GARDENS AND FARMS BECAUSE THEY RUIN IMPORTANT CROPS AND DECORATIVE GARDEN PLANTS AS THEY FEED.

SLEEPING SNAILS

Snails hibernate in the cold winter, burying in the soil and falling asleep for months. Before they hibernate, the snail seals up the entrance to its shell with a thick layer of slime, which then hardens into a tough skin. The skin protects the snail from **predators such as hedgehogs**. Air passes through a tiny hole in the skin so the snail can breathe when it is hibernating.

MEANWHILE, AT THE MOVIES...

SUPERHERO STYLE

COMIC-BOOK CHARACTERS AND ACTION HEROES WHO USE INVISIBILITY AS A SUPERPOWER INCLUDE:

INVISIBLE WOMAN
ASSUMED THE POWER OF INVISIBILITY AFTER BEING EXPOSED TO A COSMIC STORM. INVISIBLE WOMAN CAN RENDER HERSELF AND ANYONE SHE TOUCHES WHOLLY OR PARTIALLY INVISIBLE AT WILL.

PREDATOR
AN ALIEN FROM THE 1987 MOVIE OF THE SAME NAME, PREDATOR LOSES ITS INVISIBILITY POWER WHEN SUBMERGED IN WATER.

43

THE CRYOGENIC WOOLLY BEAR CATERPILLAR

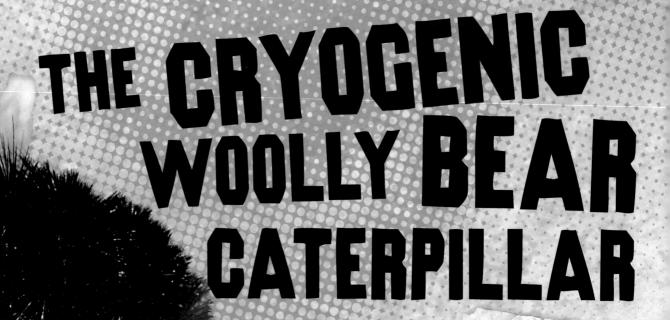

The woolly bear caterpillar is the common name given to the larva of the Isabella Tiger Moth. These moths are found throughout North America, including the bitterly cold northern part of the continent. The hardy caterpillars hibernate during the harsh Arctic winter and literally freeze solid to survive.

The woolly bear caterpillar takes its name from the **thick dense bristles, called setae,** which cover its plump body. These setae give the caterpillar a furry appearance. In fact, they help the caterpillar move by gripping the surface of the ground. Unlike many caterpillar species, the setae of the woolly bear caterpillar do not inject venom, although they may irritate your skin if you pick one up.

SUPER NATURAL POWER!

Woolly bear caterpillars hatch from eggs in the late autumn and feed constantly to bulk up their bodies. As winter approaches, the temperature drops to well below freezing. The woolly bear caterpillar stops eating, its heart slows to a standstill and the blood, guts and rest of its body **freeze solid**.

MEANWHILE, AT THE MOVIES...

SUPERHERO STYLE

COMIC BOOK CHARACTERS AND ACTION HEROES AND VILLAINS WITH CRYOGENIC SUPERPOWERS INCLUDE

FROZONE
APPEARS IN THE 2004 MOVIE THE INCREDIBLES. FROZONE IS A LONG-TIME FRIEND OF MR. INCREDIBLE AND HAS THE POWER TO FREEZE WATER AT WILL, TRAVELLING AROUND ON CHUTES OF ICE.

MR FREEZE
THIS VILLAIN WEARS A CRYOGENIC SUIT TO SURVIVE AND PLANS HIS CRIMES AROUND THE THEMES OF ICE AND COLD. MR FREEZE IS ONE OF BATMAN'S ARCH-ENEMIES.

AWESOME!
THE CATERPILLARS WILL SPEND JUST FIVE PER CENT OF THEIR LIVES FEEDING AND UP TO 90 PER CENT IN THEIR FROZEN STATE.

CHEMICAL PROTECTION

Most animals would literally freeze to death, but a chemical called a cryoprotectant **protects the caterpillar in its frozen state**. In the spring, when the temperatures rise, the caterpillar gently thaws out and its **heart starts beating again**. The caterpillar is then ready to pupate, wrapping a silk cocoon around its body and transforming into the adult Isabella Tiger moth (right).

WOW!
THE LIFE CYCLE OF THE ISABELLA TIGER MOTH TAKES 14 YEARS FROM EGG TO ADULT.

GLOSSARY

abdomen The end part of an insect's body, after the head and thorax.

antivenin A chemical that is used to treat venomous bites and stings.

bioluminescence The ability of some living things to emit light and glow in the dark.

camouflage A tactic animals use (by changing colour or shape) to blend in with their surroundings.

carnivore An animal that only eats meat.

cocoon A silky case spun by the larvae of many insects to protect them as they transform into adult insects.

colony A group of animals that live together.

cryoprotectant A chemical that prevents the bodies of living things from freezing to death.

enzyme A chemical that speeds up chemical reactions that take place in the bodies of living things.

exoskeleton The hard outer skin of an insect or other animal.

fang The hollow tooth of an animal, such as a spider. The spider uses its fangs to inject venom into prey.

habitat The natural home of an animal.

hibernate To spend the winter months in a dormant or resting state.

invertebrate An animal without a backbone.

larva The young form of bugs that undergo complete metamorphosis.

mandibles The jaws and mouthparts of insects and other bugs.

metabolism The chemical processes that take place inside the body of an animal.

metamorphosis The gradual process of change from a young form of an animal into its adult form (such as a tadpole into a frog).

mollusc An invertebrate with a soft, unsegmented body that is usually contained within a hard shell.

nymph The young form of some invertebrates, particularly insects.

ovipositor The long tube female insects use to deposit their eggs.

parasite An organism that lives on another organism and benefits at the host's expense.

pheromone A chemical released by some living things to signal to members of the same species.

predator An animal that hunts and eats other animals.

prey An animal that is hunted and eaten by other animals.

proboscis The long sucking mouthparts of some bugs.

species A group of living things that can reproduce.

thorax The middle part of an insect's body between the head and the abdomen.

venom A poisonous secretion of an animal such as a snake, which is usually delivered by a bite.

FURTHER INFORMATION

BOOKS TO READ

Extraordinary Bugs. Leon Gray, Wayland, 2011.
Deadly Factbook: Insects and Spiders, Steve Backshall,
Orion Children's Books, 2012.
Incredible Insects. Jen Green, Armadillo Books, 2013.

WEBSITES TO VISIT

http://iloveinsects.wordpress.com
The weblog of entomology student Erika Lenz, this site is devoted to all things
insects and spiders – with some great video links, images and careers advice
for students interested in insect biology.

*http://video.nationalgeographic.co.uk/video/kids/animals-pets
kids/bugs-kids*
The National Geographic video channel has some cool video clips about bug
superpowers, including some of the species mentioned in this book – dung
beetles, fires ants and jumping spiders.

PLACES TO GO

The Natural History Museum
Cromwell Road, London SW7 5BD
http://www.nhm.ac.uk

National Museum Cardiff
Cathays Park, Cardiff, CF10 3NP
http://www.museumwales.ac.uk/en/home/

National Museum of Scotland
Chambers Street, Edinburgh, EH1 1JF
http://www.nms.ac.uk

INDEX

FLEA, PAGE 24

WIDOW SPIDER, PAGE 10